I0186161

NUKECHOES

NUKECHOES

Joe Napora

BullHead Books

For "the time being"

Published in the United States

BullHead Books
509 North Main Street / Piqua Ohio / 45356

© 2021—all rights reserved
ESBN: 978-1-7364198-3-0

Acknowledgements:

"When the Fan Shits the Hit", "The Shadow of Your Smile",
"Box Cars", and "The Blast" published in *Mr. Cogito*"; "Wind
Wound" in *Xerolage 3*; "Insurance is Part of the Problem"
and "Atomic Organic Gardening" in *Quick Brown Fox*; "Little
Man the Elder" and "Wind Wound" in *Butthole Blues*.
"Rebuke" was published as a broadside by Salient Seedling
Press, Kathy Kuhen.

Cover and interior graphics by the author.

Too

late

NUCLEAR: It Happens

"Too late" came in before "not enough"
and the long term end before the snack
in the long-stay dancing school.

J. H. Prynne: *News of the Warring Clans*

happens

It happens before you
think of the word what
was that word? The very
word eluded your memory
seemed to run continually
before your grasp
                              through
        half the night and all
the while riding to
work causing you
                    to forget
to tell your son good-bye
good-bye and you leave
your bridge tokens you
leave them next to the alarm
clock

or

or it happens after
it happens
while you dream and it
enters the dream to flatten
every image into a gale
of razor blades pursuing you as you
leap in slow motion from
a cliff top and hope

for

for the first time

you will not
awaken before you hit bottom...

and you do wake for an instant
long enough
        to desire entrance back
into the nightmare and the pleasure
of that security of a hurricane
made from

from

metal and madness

it happens as you shit your muscles
worried into a spasm of fire from
the day's diarrhea and in an instant
of dread before opening the body
to the light

       instead of a quick
flash of the news of your life
in review with time to say
"Yes, after all it was good," you think
only of how you should tuck
your shoulders to soften the pain
when you dive into the bathtub

it

                              it
happens at the exact moment a car
door slams and you are carried
from your temporary conquest
of a fright that nags your body's
every sudden movement
                              each day's
unexpected sound carried with you
into an imprint of noise
fused in the cement of your driveway
leaving you speechless in your rage

it
happens

it happens as you
          close your eyes and the image
that cluttered your vision becomes
imprinted on your retina until it
melts into a swirl of line
and color where all images are mixed into
a self-indulgent fantasy of un-fulfilled
desire for some thing other than
the reflection of self loving

as you

                              it happens as
the media made atomic buddhist chants
OM and OM until he fills the Bomb
he fills the Bomb until

it bursts until it bursts and you
and you and all sensation and skin
scattered to an endless outward
race for
              an instant only an instant of
pop nirvana it happens while you

it

hap

pen

s

watch your lover drive off with
another woman and instead of wishing
both of them dead consumed in a fire
ball of gasoline and oil and plastic
seeing reruns of late night movies and
daytime soap operas

                  you feel relieved
and wish yourself well and you sprout
wings of feathers and determination
and begin to rise above the world
of dirt
         and desire above the world
of imposed responsibilities and
as your toes flutter inches above
the earth you see the light the
terrible light

it
happens

it happens at those movies
when your gaze pierces
the blankness between the projected
images and you see that motion is
both emptiness and stillness combined
in a predictable sequence until
that moment when everything becomes
a random happening of
the endless repetition
of dying it happens

it
happens

as you think of butterflies and generals
in the youth of their passions consumed
by the appetites that will transform
them into angels of frivolity and
pestilence

it
happens

it happens as all those
technicians of the sacred technological
breakthroughs invite you into
their respite from pushing the myth
of progress onward and upward and
you see them laugh and frolic as
fauns and satyrs before

                                        their skin
blisters and melts revealing metal
skeletons and tubes and wires that
hiss and crackle and snap
                    it happens

it
happens

after your son pisses the bed for
the fifth night in a row and you
stumble in the dark over his toys
and while pulling off his sheets
you rip the nail of your thumb
and before you curse before you
damn your fate for a week of
lost sleep before your cry wakes
your son who you carried to the couch
you notice

        the sky lights up with a
foreign brilliance in the west
and you realize that it is a sunset
replacing dawn or you've been sleepwalking
through the day or you've been dreaming or
you're dead it happens

it
happens

in the space
between two syllables of a word
you have wasted the afternoon
the first cool afternoon in six weeks
six weeks of heat and humidity
turning damp into mildew and the juice
your child spilled into a black and green
mold but as the breeze

and the dry cooling
are not noticed as half of a word sticks
like a clotted mass of putrid flesh in
your throat and you gag on the world
evaporating from you

it
happens

it happens before you
get to the end of the murder mystery
and before you realize the most
magnificent murder ended you and
that we all did it and that it is
no mystery it happens not
when we are crouched listening at
the radio with nerves

tightening into
a frenzy with underarms and crotch
wet with anticipation and adrenaline
quickening the breath momentarily in
communion with our mutual fear

"not
enough"

Fear

UNCLEAR: Backwards Variations

Did you ever read one of her Poems backward,
because the plunge from the front overturned?
I sometimes (often have, many times) have—
A something overtakes the Mind
                    —Emily Dickenson
          (from a note on a wrapping paper)

Look

Fear, mutual—
our communion
in momentary breath. In & out.
In & out. In. In.
                    The quickening

and adrenaline and anticipation
with wet crotch and underarms
with frenzy into tightened nerves
with radio.

Active
listening. Highly charged
are we not? Busy go
getters for the best
deal (my friend, deal). When it happens.

Backwards

Sdrowkcab

Mystery—
no, is it that?
Did all we and you ended?

Murder most magnificent. Murder most.
To get you
before it happens.

it
happens

You—from the evaporating world gag.
You and throat.
Your flesh flash.
Putrid mass

clotted, like sticks and neon
words half noticed not cooling.
Dry. Brittle. Swallow. Glass
tinkling into the gullet.

These words are added. They hurt
more. The breeze, the mold.
Green and black into a spilled child.
Into a spilled child your juice and
mildew into damp. Turning

humidity and heat of
six weeks six weeks.
Have you a word of syllables? Two,
between space. This race
to nothing. Do you
get it? To have it

is to half it.

it
happens

It happens.
That we want it all.
Fall.

Down.
Dead.

Are you dreaming?
Sleepwalking? On and on.
Dawn replacing sunset,
is it that? The symbols
are reversed. Does it
hurt more? Is it
that?

it
happens

Realize, you and the west, the very best
in brilliance of foreign light.

You.   /   Where?
Who.   /   Are you?

Son wakes, cry before sleep.
Lost fate. Last date. Crack
in the plate swallows him.
He's gone.

it
happens

Birds pray
damn you curse you
thumb nail rip you
toys dark stumble you.
It doesn't last long enough
to become an irritation.
An itch not relieved
by the scratching.

Well, it happens

it
happens

Snap and crackle and hiss that wires
you and tubes and skeletons and metal
revealing melts, blisters, skin sore
opening before satyrs and fauns fro
lic and laugh. You believe that that

is possible?

it
happens

You. Demand certainty. A tight fit.
Now aspire
to be a survivor.

Upward and onward this progress of myth,
pushing for respite
in you in you in you
infinite breakthroughs. More
physical than you expected. The joke
is on you

know who. On
top of, a last furtive
humping. As it happens
the dirty old men at the peep show laughing.

Pestilence and frivolity of angels
transform will, appetites, the
consumed passions, their youth,
generals and butterflies.

it
happens

As it happens.

Dying of repetition.
Endless happenings random.
Old habits unbroken.
Become everything
in combined stillness

and emptiness. Both.
You and images
projected
between blankness.

The pierces gaze you
when it happens.

Light, terrible light. See.
The oldest image
the most terrible.

it
happens

Imposed world above desire and dirt. Fuck it.
Determination and feathers of wings, sprout.
Just try it. Sprout.
Sprout. It is not enough.
You are not Daedalus. Pluck. Pluck.

A melodrama in a night of reruns. Run.
Seeing plastic and oil and gasoline
fireball, consumed dead. Then. Where run?

You run rerun
while it happens.

it

happens

Nirvana. Pop. Race outward, endless
scattered skin and sensation—all.
And you. And you. And

bursts, bursts.

Bomb. Bomb.
Oh o.
Butterflies and bees gone to vapor.
As it happens.

it
happens

Self loving reflection.
Indulgent self

into mixed images
where color and line swirl
into melt. Mirrors as weapons.
Until retina imprinted becomes vision.
Your clotted image wishes for darkness.

The eyes close.

You.
As it happens.

it
happens

Rage. Speechless. You
leaving driveway of cement in
fused noise of imprint into you
with carried sound unexpected.

Should you only think good after all?
Yes. Review life. Flash. Quick.
Light the body opening
before dread.

Day's fire spasm
into worried muscles.
Your shit. As
it happens.

it
happens

Madness and metal
from made hurricane of security
and pleasure and nightmares.

Into black entrance desire enough
a long instant, motion slow. Leap
pursuing blades, gale of images
enter you. You've swallowed the
projector and willingly.
While it happens.

it
happens

After.

Leave tokens. You.
Last traces. It is hardly
something. More like a
nothing.

Good bye son.
All night continually that memory
eluded that word.
The word?
What was that word?
That was what word?

The?

Of?

Think.

No. That that
is hard.

Before it happens.

Before

NUKE LEAR

I stumbled when I saw
King Lear

'L'eer

Look Leukemia

It is not the starlet's lips dripping
cream and honey nor the tanned
muscleman with sand kicked in
the face of the pimp voyeur
that demands permanence. Nothing

sticks to your ribs. Eve to vapor.
Eve the ghostie rising.
Out of sight. Outta site.

Adam turned to a suckling pig
even with eyes closed and breast
flesh pressed near nose
saw through skin to the bone.

Negative.
Negative.

Retina groans.

Jocular & Oracular Were Sweethearts

It is not enough
to say stuff it

you piss-complectioned turd-bloated
money-suckin politician skunksniffer.

Nor is it enough
to pretend to smell roses
through the sewer gas.

First. Act.

The future was once
as solid as fact. So? No
joke. The punch
line bombed.

The Revenge of the Body Snatchers

The projectionist was a poet
with a humor sensed
into an ache balanced
by nonsense. Get it?

He did.

He played the film in reverse
to see the dead resurrect whole
as the final and worst curse
from the mouths of the ghouls.

Piss on Myth

It is the sign that flashes
in the mind what crashes
as a car tumbles.   Melts.
Is what he mumbles.

Whose fault is it? Oil
slick on the highway
rush hour. A chain
reaction. If

that sign ahead said
This Is The End
Of The Highway Proceed
At Maximum Entropy

then you may take your place satisfied
that the crunch of metal you occupy
is some atomic scientist's
future favorite music.

Technogenic Disease in the Anti-War Poem

The soldiers were also victims
so muzzle your meanness.
The poets are part of the lymph system
carrying wastes out not eating them.

So much for rime.
All the talk of poets
means less this time.

The lilting voice
the magic presence,
the atoms of Homer's body
dispersed through time

breathed into the voice
of the modern bard, exits
with the blood through the ears.
Here.

Television Repairman and the Electron Gun

A story of my father distorted
by the presence of an alien medium.
He warned my sister and me
never to sit too close
not to stare too long at the tv.

He also used to swear at magazine
peddlers and wasn't fond of books.
He said he could tell better stories.
And he did. I remember

his fear as I saw through him
the time the news showed the bomb
of course it was not real but a model
of the one dropped on the Hiroshima

and he put his body
before the screen.
Then the light
went out.

Dreaming Leviathan

The most frightening nightmares
were not the recurring flight
aided by the flutter of arms
enabling me to leap and float
from the houses in the project
to telephone poles to houses
to poles watch the wires
that slipped, sagged to the ground.
The enormous weight.
The ooze of earth. No.

The nightmares were abstract.
Brown shapes squeezed
into a room and me there
a small I and the sound
of their rubbing like
an amoeba wearing
a suit of sandpaper.

Who's looking?
I guess.
I was.

Insurance is Part of the Problem

The way the ground swells or your mouth
from the shock accepts the surprise
of your favorite broken stereo
types is a sign that gutted speech

is the main design but
there is no time to learn
the sad sermon's truth. There
is no guarantee
we will ever dream within the
distortion of springtime
no guarantee
our Sunday stroll is not gone

forever. The bombs fell on the cities.
With no place to walk, no sights
to see except in the suburbs with lots
of space still and available
for a price for the future
underground cemeteries.

Plaster deer. Plastic flowers.
Holding lanterns black jockies
painted white. Pink flamingoes.
Flamingoes. Oh.
Flamingoes.

Wind Wound

The acceptance of fabricated value
with an exaggerated interest
compounded by the finger dance
upon some flunky's calculator
doesn't add to my peace of
mind nor to any beggar's
collection plate just the
transcendental butt fucker
taking his pleasure upon
the confused minions bent
before the gold sequined calf.

Little Man the Elder

An old buzzard laced with wisdom
forged from morphine substitutes and
a bank account grafted on the loose
skin of his thighs sighs.

Should he retreat from the surf roar?
Will he challenge the hardening of habit?

The action is elsewhere.
A dog who eats the ocean spray
and a young naked couple
are making commercials for diet cola
while the chug chug
of the producing line continues.

Rock Video

The bankers are the ultimate socialists
straining at a leash tied to the axis
joining North and South poles
pushing paper money on everyone.

The leash turns.
The fire burns.
The pole grease slips
and various holes
stuffed up and shut

which is the true aim
of cost accounting. Only
the weight of stones will save us
cries the tenured professors.
But even the liberals fear the golden rule
will turn on us. Go electric.
Go electric.

Cut the balls for the illusion
of a deeper penetration.

The kids are watching tv
and turn up the volume.

Mom is in the bedroom with the Tarot.
Only for a moment did they think
they heard her crying.

Atomic Organic Gardening

It is more than compost
more than clay loam mixed
with leaf mold, scraps, shit

more than the sweet scent
of the inevitable
that pulls you

down, breaks you under foot
into a minute confusion
of a process you thought

you understood, breaks you into
worm mouth, devouring
detached penises with minds

of their own, relentlessly
eating only stopping to speak
for you. That is the attraction.

Moneybags Moneyego 1984

The wait of a tradition gone
to distant shores. There
is no record of stone
money being tied about

the neck of a man condemned.
Instead they sacrificed millstones and
the lenders sold the millers on the need
for new ones. Sure, there is no free

lunch. But the ones who say that
don't mean it. Lewis Strauss
said electricity made from atomic power
would be so cheap you wouldn't need

to meter it. But the foot either measures
or falls on you. Forever.

Children of the Fat Man Free Verse

Money is only the movement
of electrons lighting a display
for your satisfaction.   And you
only the play

of the atoms spent
by the wreck of a too concentrated
capital. So there is no longer
any problem about taking it with you

when you die. To bankroll
the apocalypse is the happy con
sequence of the mercantile logic
leaving no lips

left to abuse your
money or your memory.

When the Fan Shits the Hit

Claude Eatherly flew his plane, a B-29 name
Straight Flush, over Hiroshima looking for a hole
in the clouds so the bombardier of the Enola Gay
could find his target....
                          Thomas Shaffer, *Countdown Zero*

Only a piece of baked dirt
to think he could win
could claim medical benefits
for the dizziness and nausea
after flying into that hot cloud
just one very naive son of a gun
a very silly clod
hopper who finally turned
into a petty criminal turned
into a piece of baked dirt
in a hospital for the insane
who dreamed of his own name
dropped into a hole that sucked him in
to a twist of fate leading
to a descending darkness of a spiral
spiraling beyond his control in
a game called madness and meanness
where he is finally crushed
in an incoherence of a roar of the loss
of a sure thing like love like duty
pulled down by a straight flush.

This One Poem I Cannot Write

It should be easy to write a poem
about John Wayne,
the media's Uncle Sam,
Captain Red, White, and Blue,
Tough Talker, Tall Walker,
Mr. Rugged Individual,
Mr. Misterman Himself filming
a movie called *The Conqueror*
at Snow Canyon a spot hot
from fallout. Why when cancer conquers him

does nothing come from
the irony, the symbolism, the paradox inherent
in this story?   John Wayne the model
for the myriad of unknown soldiers
the very soldiers killed like he was

by these tests. The Conqueror.   I repeat.
Perhaps this poem will be salvaged
not savaged by history.
"el" oh "el"
The missing irony.
The missing "el."

WEap

on

on

on

FLUKE

Weapons always defeat the poor who receive
them. Only the brick and the stick a man
picks up in anger will not defile him as a man.

—Francisco Juliao

The Blast

During the next sixteen
Weeks, Kelly and his men walked to the lagoon
to witness Armageddon. They
Endured the penetrating light
That, for one long moment was all that
existed, felt the searing heat,
heard the long, rolling thunder,
steadied themselves for the shock
waves and winds, were awed by
the ascending fireball of colors
and flames, experienced the

Dwarfing scale of the blasts and their own feelings
of insignificance, and they knew a
penetratin horror. But they could not
sense the
Radiation. They witnessed Butternut, and Wahoo, and
Holly, and Yellowwood, and Magnoia, and
Tobacco, and Rose, and Umbrella, and
Walnut. The men went to the dark shores
of Japan and saw the rising suns of Linden and
Elder,
And Oak, and Sequoia, and Dogwood, and Scaerola,
and Pisonia and Olive, and Pine, and
Quince, and Fig. The
Men watched a nuclear blast every three days. Once
there were two
Shots in a day.

Box Cars

The lead B29 took its name
From its customary pilot, Fred Bock,
And a winged and punning boxcar painted
                    on its fuselage. On
This occasion he happened, however, to be
                    flying the instrument plane

Called The Great Artiste. But the weather did
                    not permit nor was God apparently
                    willing that Kokura should enter the
History books. He
Abandoned Bock's Car's primary objective and
                    turned toward's the secondary alternative
Nagasaki. "Fat Man" fell....It fell for forty
                    seconds. And in the forty seconds
                    every move that people
Chose to make below became of vital importance,
                    a choice between life and death, between
                    degrees of pain and grief. 500 meters
                    above the city the bomb detonated. It was
11.02 a.m.

Styx and Stone, Bryx and Bones

1.

Three journalists who
Had
Escaped

Their death had paid a boatman, piled into
         his leaky vessel, and had been
Rowed, the first argonauts of the atomic age,
         down one of those rivers so choked
         with the dead and dying that the
         boatman had difficulty getting his oar
Into the water. The three were Bin Nakamura, Kaoru
         Katashima, and Tadashinge Maehara, and
         they were reporters for Domei, the
         Japanese news agency, whose motto, it
         should be noted, was
"Patriotism Through Journalism."

2.
         There
Were thousands of dead bodies bobbing
All around
They were so burned and scorched that
         you couldn't
Even tell whether they were men or women.
         I thought I was floating down a
River in hell.

3.

Suddenly one of them stuck up
Out of the water
          and the hand grabbed onto the
Side of the boat.

4.
          But the
Skin came
Off in
Sheets.

5.
          He took but five pictures
          and none of them
Shows the dead.
He couldn't bring himself to shoot them,
          and what he did shoot, he told me,
          after hours of walking around the
          city, he shot through a veil
Of
Tears and to the
Sounds of his own prayers for forgiveness.

6.
　　　All the paper in the
City had been vaporized or burned.
　　　Journalism couldn't
Exist because there was
Nothing to print on. What was left
　　　of the newspaper
Staff just went into the streets
　　　to shout
Out the news...
　　　Japanese journalism has
　　　developed in
Response to the Japanese experience
　　　of nuclear war.

7.
　　　The entire nuclear regime, in fact,
　　　is both an organization of
Violence and an
Organization of knowledge.
It is a system that maintains deterrence by
　　　mobilizing science, technology
　　　industry, and politics. But it is
　　　also a system that sustains itself
　　　by organizing the knowledge that all
　　　this other activity requires. The
　　　nuclear regime, in other words, has
　　　its own epistemological structure,
　　　its own set of possibilities for
　　　acquiring knowledge. This structure
　　　was designed by the Manhattan Project,
　　　strengthened at the time of the Hiroshima
　　　bombing, and
Cemented
Every year thereafter.

8.

The cognitive possibilities
structured by the
Nuclear regime
Establish
What may be known,

And by whom; a definition of
Secrecy

And accessibility; a

Politics of
Information and a
Media
Politics.

9.

The epistemological structure
defines fields of inquiry
And determines their
Relationship one
To the other.

It
Sets the

Agenda for scientific and medical research.
It establishes the

Dr. Teller Told Him "Young fella' better fold 'em"

In a 1978 testimony to the House
Subcommittee on Health and the Environment,
Dr. Teamplin described how the Atomic
Energy Commission had blocked his work
and made him a "non-
Person" after his complaints about nuclear
Energy. In similar fashion, Dr. Irwin Bross,
the chief biostatistician at
Roswell Park
Memorial Institute, the nation's oldest cancer
research center,

A few years ago complained the
National Cancer Institute was exposing women
under age fifty to a foolhardy cancer
risk by enrolling large numbers of them
in experimental breast-cancer screening
programs that included an annual mamo-
gram or breast X ray; the National
Cancer Institute revoked the funding it
had supplied Roswell Park for nine years--
and with this move ended one of the
very few research programs anywhere that
focused on
Damage from

Diagnostic X rays. Actually, not
Even
A Nobel Prize has proved to be protection
against such harassment. In 1955, for
example, the United States delegation to
the Geneva "Atoms for Peace" Conference
exquisitely embarrassed itself by, at
The last moment, forbidding Dr.
Herman Muller, the geneticist who had discovered
the mutagenicity of X rays, to deliver his
scheduled talk on the adverse effects of
radiation.

Exit to Reno

I did not know that there were dogs,
Monkeys, burros,
And
Pigs

Positioned at various distance from the bomb's
hypocenter. The pigs had been dressed
In military uniforms and placed behind
Glass
Shields. Officials from the Defense Department

Wanted to use the pigs
In a simulated
Test of blast effects on a uniformed man standing
erect, but for months their determined
efforts to train the pigs to stand on
their
Hind legs had met with only disinterested grunts.
When the bomb was detonated, the
problem was solved.

A moment of terror accomplished what months of
training could not. The pigs not
only stood erect but leaped over
the enclosure fences as particles of

100

Glass drove deep into their bodies....
At
Zero, I heard a loud click. Immediately I felt
an intense heat on the back of my
neck. A brilliant flash accompanied
the heat, and I was shocked when, with
my
Eyes tightly closed, I could see the bones

In my forearms as though I were examining
a red x-ray. I learned many years
later that I had been x-rayed by
force many times greater than a
Normal medical x-ray. Within seconds, a

Thunderous rumble like the sound
Of thousands of stampeding cattle passed

directly overhead, pounding the
trench line. Accompanying the
roar was an
Intense pressure that pushed me downward.
The shock wave was travelling at
Nearly four hundred miles per hour
pushed toward us by the immense
energy of the explosion. The
Sound and the pressure were both frightening
And deafening. The earth began to gyrate
violently, and I could
Not see four feet in front of me. I could
not locate the person who had
been nearest to me in the trench.
A light many times brighter than
the sun penetrated the thick
dust, and I imagined that some
Evil force

Was attempting to swallow my body and soul.
I thought the world was coming
to an end. I was certain that,
with the raging, angry shaking
of the earth, the very ground
beneath me would be rent asunder.
If what I was experiencing was
an example
Of nuclear war, I wanted no part of it. I
saw no way that friend or foe,
marine or foreign adversary could
survive such an experience. As
the initial sound wave bounced
off the surrounding mountains and
Returned, we were struck by a second shock
wave. A loud noise comparable to a
tremendous clap of thunder made me
cringe. The trembling of the earth
mercifully ended at last. I had been
bounced helplessly around in the
trench for ten to twelve seconds
that seemed like an eternity. I felt as
though I have been attacked and
savagely beaten by a gang of toughs
who hammered on my helmet and tore
at my clothing from all sides. I
was alive but
Dazed. No one had prepared me for what I had
experienced. Had
Something gone wrong or was my encounter
typical of a nuclear explosion?

My Money's on Beauty, You Bet on the Beast

You have a neuromuscular disorder. I don't
concur with the doctor who diagnosed
myashina gravis, but our tests
Show
A definite abnormality. I don't know what
Caused your condition or how far it will progress.
There is no treatment, and I cannot tell
you if it will ever
Regress.   We will just have to watch you.
If you reach a point where you can't
Function, we have plenty of beds here at the hospital.
Just don't ask me to get
Involved in this radiation
Controversy, because
I won't. Consider yourself
And the others from the test site who are
Ill as the few who sacrificed yourselves for the
many who were spared.

Then he asked, "Would you tell me
where I
Can get copies
Of those
Photographs
You showed me? (the Priscilla and Hood explosions).
I think the colors are beautiful, and I
want to put them on my office wall."

The Shadow of Your Smile,
The Smile of Your Shadow

When we sailed
Into
Nagasaki harbor, we crowded to the port side of
        the ship

And craned our
Necks for a view. We looked for human life--
        there was none. We saw total
Devastation. The major buildings were nothing
        but skeletons....

Later we were moved to a schoolhouse.
        At ground zero I saw a phenomenon which
        I could not comprehend. I saw the shadow
Of a man on a brick wall with nothing else around
        and no man to make the
Shadow. I realize now that this shadow had to
        have been a human being who was fused
        to the wall at the time of the
Explosion of the atom bomb.

Sources

"The Blast" from *Countdown Zero* by Thomas H. Saffer and Orville E. Kelly, New York: 1982.

"Box Cars" from *Nagasaki 1945* by Tatsuichiro Akizuki,New York: 1981.

"Styx and Stones..." from "The Silence" by RobertKarl Manoff, in *The Quill,* Feb. 1984.

"Dr. Teller..." from *At Highest Risk* by Christopher Norwood, New York: 1980.

"Exit to Reno," "My Money's on Beauty..." and "The Shadow of Your Smile..." from *Countdown Zero.*

THE STONE NUKULELE

I aimed my Pebble—but Myself
Was all the one that fell—
Was it Goliath—was too large--
Or was myself —too small?
                —Emily Dickinson

Shore and Sea is Five—hearts,
clubs, spades, diamonds. joker

The Knave is Two

Threes the flowing

Three—the stream

Fours—is the Joker

The Suits, the Seasons are One

Shore and Sea is Five
   —hearts, clubs, spades, diamonds, joker

Knots upon the star lit dreams
of money, hard cash, for the face
pressed into the shingles is tied
to dying. A scene cut
from "On the Beach." The hero

the hero speculates on rock & roll
the music and the voice he once called his
own his not petrified onto a record long
since washed overboard in the sea wreck.
Where is his guitar? Where?

The pressure of tiny stone smoothed
smoothed by the sea wash dug from
the sea's embrace filling the stone scars
stone scars in a strand
a strand slips about his neck

...and that Dylan he remembers
hearing it while walking through the
Latin Quarter of Paris the echoes, concrete
concrete and cobbles "Everybody must get stoned...."
and, of course, the magic of thee Stones

with words ablaze and the hunger of those blues
guitars but the stones he speculates on
and on and into this pressure of the life ebb
in themselves mean nothing. Solidity
is but a makeshift virtue. The rocks

at Carnac, the henges, circles,
the rocks lifted, labored into precision
the rocks, the henges, patterns, circles are still
standing and resist the ultimate, the ultimate
melt for they uphold an idea that sustains them. Us.

Such is the design of a song this song
never to be played upon any imagined
imagined guitar and rocks, pebbles, boulders,
all, free as we refuse to be
to be as solid as the recurring dream

to be to dream the possibilities
the body knows in its wrack upon a shore
a wreckage of wonder why
why these intimate injuries of heads split, spheres
called dreams dreams of these eggs broken.

The Knave is Two
—to/fro, me/you, fe/fo

Cracks. As any egg must eventually
and the ooze of life inevitably.

It is larger than life how the stone,
the pebble fits easily between thumb

and finger, finger thumb, a lucky charm worn
by constancy and fear, how the hand

gives a lie to the mind's complacent
immediacy and evokes the cosmic egg.

The wonder of the mess contained
in yolk is obvious to all but the shell

the shell is discarded from thought.
But the shell of the stone is its hell

is its home. Humpty must fall and all
the King's horses and men, all silence

the opposition. Then something else this
something breaks. The bourgeoisie tremble still

at the sight of the stone in the hand
the hand of the un-repentant youth.

There is a folk belief that a cure
for "the shakes" is to hold a stone in

the hand hold the hand out until the arm
the arm tires the muscle trembles until fatigue

fatigue kills the urge this urge to turn the body's heat
its natural and blessed dispensation inward

inward against itself but out now out
outward with cool determination. The motion

that motion could be stopped by photographic
techniques of of a thousand separate pictures

pictures hung on a wall hung in a museum and the pictures
pictures replacing stages of the growth of mushroom

clouds about this boy showing a revived
progression of the flight of the missile the

missile leaving his hand approaching the head
of the policeman (these still photos caught

caught and sliced manage to give us time
we manage to take that time

to replace the figure of the policeman
with that of the *Guardia*, Spain of Franco,

Nicaragua of Somoza) and even the crack
the crack as it opens in the head and

and the juice this juice
of the blood flows. The juice.

Threes the flowing

Stones are difficult to exchange just as hard
to take back a word spoken (not quite
broken but hard even if no one hears

as it leaves a path or trace to follow)
the rhyme is hollow leaving me
leaving me to wonder from this stone

that is really cheese to see how these giants
they do fall if they can be tricked and they
these giants can and they do. Our history

our history as it is hidden is our strength
strength that is hidden and our hope for
for it was meant never to be a fair

a fair fight and the giant's might and
his arrogance did also impress the other
giants when between his fingers the juice

fell hot not his sweat but the water
he squeezed from the stone. Such super
power has a compelling logic of terror that

has an admiration due it. And did the tailor
this tailor who confused his words and was
rewarded did he cheat? Of course. In his hand

he calmly squeezed a piece of cheese and the whey ran
but was visible to the giant as water from
the disadvantage of his great height and

and then there is the more familiar story
not of the tailor but of that other that
incongruity of Goliath and David.

Three

—the stream

The cure for madness practiced by the
Indians of Peru is for the possessed
to sit by a stream and throw stones into it

until eventually he throws out the
madness and is cured and I
immediately think of the career

bureaucrats who ache for to push
the button that will bring on the very
last war for them to believe for ten

minutes they finally are cured also
and I also think about
the tribes living downstream and picture

a woman washing her family's clothes
in the stream which washed the stones
thrown by the madmen at Three Mile Island.

Fours

—is the Joker

It is the tailor again and was
it luck that he picked up the bird
and placed it in his pocket? Doubtful
given that St. Francis has a legacy.

In the contest with the giant he threw
the bird pretending it to be a stone
and the bird flew out of sight well
beyond the giant's throw and the giant

must have found it hard to see since
a flying bird looks little like a thrown
stone perhaps he was expecting something
worse and wanted not to look too closely

at the tailor or the stone perhaps
perhaps giants have a learned genetic code
and stones remind them of David's message and
they see the stone in its release

and in a stopped motion approaching
in steps of accelerated violence they
see the stone approach Goliath
and in the pass between the eyes

as it makes contact with the forehead
they then are Goliath and their shadow
races from the horizon to meet them not
to cushion their fall to the ground nor

the echo of the Boss's image pulled
from the pedestal now only rubble piled
in the streets of Warsaw. Not the glint
of the sun flash from the steel blinded

the giant to the movement of the bird's
wings but the fear of the shadow confused
him as he imagines it sweeping across him
in a ritualistic move even before

even before he toppled—the glint, the glint—
before he toppled—the glint—
toppled and then the downward arc
of the sword.

The Suits, the Seasons are One

In one form of another it is always the same religion
of beauty, this stupid "goddess," mute as a dream in
stone; the justification for so much fanaticism and
the pretext for so much cowardice
          —Jacques Ehrmann, "The Death of Literature"

There are form of songs abbreviated

and just cannot be mediated by design

forced into fake fullness when

the player learns to level expectations

to respect the obvious limits of his

instrument. Eventually the labor comes to

fruition and the onlookers are then

redeemed in spite of their reluctance

if they learned however painfully

to attune their bodies to a truncated

music. And the music is a gesture

not freely given but taken from the picture

painted in 1849 the year after the year

of defeat the year we still live by the

same year he sketched "The Burial at Ornans"

and it shows two men stopped in a moment

of working with the one arrested

in time as he is about to bring down

the hammer. You can see the veins popped
on his right hand, this is not a relaxed
upward stroke. His right leg is bent but
also twisted and his wooden shoe lies not
flat to the ground but this awkwardness does
not indicate his being off balance and about
to fall but that the motion of the hammer
breaking stone provides the balance. The
other supports the weight of his basket
of broken stone on his raised knee as he
grips it as if to relieve the stones for
a moment of their weight to take it upon
himself before he drops them all to make
a road that even now is being used as
it extends beyond the picture painted by
Corbet called "The Stonebreakers."

Puke

PUKE
—the atomic alphabet

(for Xhlebnikov
the trace of his butterfly)

The
echo

A melt begins
And a melt begins
Against things solid and
Antagonistic like stone
Angels words right
Angles for the

Bomb is
Boy o boy is
Bang bang and suffer the little

Children do not escape the
Conflagration for it is
Crucial at the
Culmination there be this
Crescendo of
Cries that
Continues but

Death is only a big
Disappointment if we all are
Damned we lose the
Delight of
Dividing gods from
Demons though

Everyone weeps while the
Evening continues to
Envelop the

Entrance to the
End the
Evangelists
Envisioned as an
Excellent moneymaking
Enterprise as the

Fierce voice calls
Fee
Fie
Foe Ho Hum the minister

Gesticulates
Gee the
Giant has a
Gentle
Grasp

Here is
How it
Happens
Invent an

I that
Increases
Indefinitely

Just

Killing and killing and

Last but not
Least the travelling
Light
Leveling not
Little by little but
Less and
Less and
Less with

More heat than
Most imagine with
Molecules and
Money forever fixed in a
Montage of a commercial
Message repeated by a privileged
Minority we can now call a
Monster of greed's
Making

Nerves and
Neutrons shadowed into a
Nothing so profound with
No one remaining to
Nudge the sleeper

On to better things as

Proud males
Posing in
Particularly menacing
Postures
Propelling meaning of
Pricks swollen and
Pointed to
Pierce to
Pieces

Quiet don't tell on them
Quit complaining you will be
Quite handsomely

Rewarded with
Real and
Red fragments mixing a
Roar of crazed
Reason proclaiming the

Rush into the abstract
Regimen

Sell your
Soul it's gone

The body's
Thrust propels it against
Thin glass
Tinkle muffled in blood

Up against the wall
U r de wall

Very much gone

Whiter than
White

X-ray for free for ever

Yes it is all ground

ZerOh

R E B U K E D

It seems comical and miserable that in order to
manifest itself, dread, which opens and closes the sky,
needs the activity of a man sitting at his table and
forming letters on a piece of paper.

—Maurice Blanchot

1. On Her Some Thing Is Falling

Name a word wrap about
yourself like a sentence stretched
to protect your face from cuts
and bruises brought for you
to apply like makeup to
please the purveyors of new fashion.
Name a word that wounds
knowing it now has a life of sound
beyond your control beyond care
beyond longing except for the buyers
who take it and sharpen the image
drill it deep into you for
a price you willingly pay.
Name a word and watch
it live a life of its own
not hung about the human predicament
but free to wander aimlessly
until it too becomes an agent
in some power passion play.

These are cartoon figures I write of.
They are not flesh nor skeleton only
nor stick figures mocking completion.
Cut from the Sunday newspaper
any man and any woman joined
at the feet with a clip perhaps
mounted on cardboard reinforced
to insure long pleasure, pleasure
of a rather abstract sort, and a
hand pushing the man down on
and into this approximate woman
and up again and down this man

who slowly fills out in color and
in form, becomes a rounded out
character swollen and bulging at
the junction of his legs, sprouting
missiles inching forward at
each thrust of this hand as
it works through its boredom
and its malice filling this woman
all the while that it cuts her.

2. She, For a Price, Accepts Her Calling

Again the images are really only
cartoon figures animated on a screen
by a frustrated painter who painfully
draws each frame for a film
in the solitude of a reverie he
is determined to share with us.
The woman who gains a sort of life
beneath his pen is taken by
two men who handle each leg and
pump them as if she is a sort
of bellows and from her fly
those very same missiles charged
with a particular poison that
substitutes for an enforced silence.

3. Catch a Falling Star and Drop It

The scene is a television, rapidly moving
images. The scene is Latin, a body's
looseness, a moving that delighted
and shook a nation out of a rigidity
so profound it threatened paralysis.

When she moved, we rocked. We trembled.
We finally needed to form her into a
screen goddess to control our own passion
and to market these desires. Less now,
almost nothing, even the pictures in
Playboy, the pink skin against red silk sheets,,
even this fails to excite anyone anymore,
she is a symbol beyond Hollywood control.
Marilyn Monroe is Cuba. Now a certain
consistency evolves that demands its own
accuracy. It is a consistency of
the Sunday comics again. This heroic
figure threatening to blowup the world
from his throne in Camelot. In the secret
reaches of this castle are the chambers
of the president's prized courtesan.
The servants apply makeup and costumes
and instruct her in the art of waiting.
He enters, finally he enters beyond
the reach of cameras and politics.
No longer is anything subtle, no longer
is the language a style designed
to mystify. His words fill tiny balloons
that crowd each scene. The starlet
opens herself. He talks and bulges
and sprouts tiny fangs like missiles.
Next Sunday she will give her neck
to his embrace. Readers anticipate.

No After Words

1. The ad

After the day after is a nothing.
A popular television show succeeded
when the media demanded it deny that nothing.
And the advertisers applauded the absence
of that nothing.

And television cannot collect revenue
(it is like avenue, like *au revoir)*
revenue on the real apocalypse
but it can create sequels to the fake one.
The survivors will set new standards for fashion.
The survivors will create new soap operas.
The survivors will host Saturday Night Live.
The survivors will be politicians.

Joe McCarthy never died, he faded
away into advertising.
The 50s never passed on anything
but their disease. The CIA became
microbes, became carcinogens.
The virus spread through Iran in 53.
The virus spread through Guatemala in 54.
Strontium-90 made mothers fear their breasts.
At the milk company the alchemist
takes fallout and turns it into gold.

2. Cash Flow

I grew up during the 50s in the middle
of the heartland that is the ache
in the middle of the midwest
—Dayton, Ohio. I remember most
the SAC base and NCR.

The planes overhead, half of them always
in the air with their bombs. And
The National Cash Register Company's shows

on Saturdays. For a can of fruit or soup
an hour's worth of cartoons.
The air base remains.
The bombers come and go.

The cash register company has skipped town.
Soccer fields and classrooms where factories once stood.
Hiroshima, those pictures.
Gold dust spread to the four corners,
hot to the touch. Strategic
Air Command.

The men and women who filled the registers
with their worth, they are gone.
Some empty lots, they remain.

Money turned into time future,
bits of light flashing
at the end
of the sewer.

3. The vista

I remember school windows.
I remember a time when

windows were not seen
as weapons. And

I remember the A-bomb drills.
I remember the remembering

in this fear of windows.
A whole generation in a forced leap

of its imagination turned inward
replacing the windows out into the world

with brick, stone, bars of lead
to keep us distracted from the atomic dead.

You hear the stones that used to be my friend.
    —Ray Bonneville "Where Has My Easy Gone?"

The End

This is a test.

¿wHere?

Fact Sheets & Briefs

Type of Test	United States	Total
Atmospheric	215	528
Underground	815	1,528
Total	1,030[1] (Note: **does** not include atomic bombings of Hiroshima and Nagasaki.)	2,056

BullHead
Books

www.ingramcontent.com/pod-product-compliance
Lightning Source LLC
Chambersburg PA
CBHW071124090426
42736CB00012B/2003